Don't Pray For Rain And Then Complain When Your Hair Frizzes

Don't Pray For Rain And Then Complain When Your Hair Frizzes

Donna Cannon Smith

Xulon Press

Xulon Press
555 Winderley Pl, Suite 225
Maitland, FL 32751
407.339.4217
www.xulonpress.com

© 2024 by Donna Cannon Smith

All rights reserved solely by the author. The author guarantees all contents are original and do not infringe upon the legal rights of any other person or work. No part of this book may be reproduced in any form without the permission of the author.

Due to the changing nature of the Internet, if there are any web addresses, links, or URLs included in this manuscript, these may have been altered and may no longer be accessible. The views and opinions shared in this book belong solely to the author and do not necessarily reflect those of the publisher. The publisher therefore disclaims responsibility for the views or opinions expressed within the work.

Unless otherwise indicated, Scripture quotations taken from the New King James Version (NKJV). Copyright © 1982 by Thomas Nelson, Inc. Used by permission. All rights reserved.

Paperback ISBN-13: 978-1-66289-529-6
Ebook ISBN-13: 978-1-66289-530-2

Table of Contents

Who is Sharing Your Umbrella? vii
Check for Leaks Before You Put a Boat into the Water 1
Are You Listening? 7
Hidden Snakes. 11
Never Push a Drowning Victim into the Deep 17
Missing Ingredients 25
Shipwrecked on Dry Ground. 29
Opossums and Pontiacs 35
A Dog Named Budweiser 41
Cooks and Christians. 45
Blood, Bruises and the Bathtub. 49
One Step at a Time. 55
Low-Maintenance Friends 61
Quick-Moving Fog 63
Hidden Worms 67
Coloring. 71
You Can't Wipe Off Love. 73
True Love 75
It's A Matter of Choice 79
Life According to Matthew 83
Tarry Until 87
What is that Wonderful Fragrance? 91
Acknowledgements. 95

Introduction

Who is Sharing Your Umbrella?

How often in our lives do we pray for rain and then complain when our hair frizzes or fuss about the mud? Everyone gets tired of wet weather, and we say, "If only the sun would shine." Then, the sun comes out, and we are quick, to complain about the heat.

I pray that these short stories will bring a smile to your face and a thought of just how personal our God is and how much He is teaching us in our every day lives.

When my grandson was four-years-old, I remember a time when he was preaching in the backseat of our car, like only a four-year-old can do. He was sharing how God made the sun and the moon and the stars. He told us how God made all the people and all the animals. We said, "Amen, Eli, preach it!" Then he made a statement that I will forever remember. He said, "God made the rain, and then He got all wet." Then the sermon stopped and he moved onto something else.

I had never thought of God in that way. God made the rain and then He got wet. I told Eli that I believe that's probably just how it happened, because God enjoyed His creation.

We serve a personal God who is moved to compassion with the feelings of our infirmities. He loved us so much that He gave His only son so we could live with Him forever.

This same God who spoke the universe into motion and measures out Heaven with His hand, also made rabbits and bears, kittens and crocodiles.

He is the same God who gave me a revelation through a four year old that after God made the rain; He got wet.

I don't actually know if God got wet. I may be old, but I personally did not witness this event. However, I do believe we serve a personal God who enjoyed the creation of His hands, even to the point of getting wet.

When the rains of life come and we feel like the sun may never shine again, remember that God is there beside us, through the rain, getting wet.

What a loving, personal God we serve. He is not a God who is way off, but a God who will get wet with you during the storms of life.

I choose to ask God if he wouldn't mind sharing my umbrella during the rainy days and not to complain when my hair frizzes.

Chapter 1

Check for Leaks Before You Put a Boat into the Water

DESPITE THE OCCASIONAL hurricanes, we feel blessed to live in the beautiful state of Florida. In addition, we have always loved the water and a few years ago, we were fortunate enough to live on a lake.

For the first two years we lived there, we drooled as we watched other people playing on their boats and Jet Skis. However, we were content to play around the small beach at the back of our house. You would think just living on a lake would be great enough – what we would give to live back there now.

Since we were youth pastors at the time, we had to be very frugal with our limited income and could only dream of the day when God would bless us with a boat. Please don't misunderstand – God always provides for our needs and even our wants, but sometimes He wants us to be patient and content with what we have. So for two years we were content as we watched and continued to drool.

Finally, out of the clear blue sky, someone gave us a fishing boat. You would have thought he had given us a Bass Tracker or a Nitron because we were ecstatic, elated and overjoyed, to say the least. Then we actually saw the boat. It was definitely not a Ski Nautique or a Master Craft like they use at Cypress Gardens. However, it was a boat and we were so thankful.

Once we saw it, we were much too gracious to complain. We had wanted a boat and someone gave us one. Who gives a boat away? The motor was in great shape and we are forever thankful for the generosity of a dear friend. However, it did need a little bit of work.

Anyway, we were tickled and my husband spent endless hours working on this boat to get it into tiptop shape to take on the lake. He put in a new floor, new seats and new carpet. However, the boat still leaked.

Grant it we had never really owned a boat large enough to have a motor. So the thought of a boat with more than one plug was foreign to us. (I can see all of you boat owners shaking your heads in disbelief – don't judge!)

After all the work my husband had put into the boat, my well-meaning husband convinced me to take a maiden voyage on the boat. He said "I think I have repaired all the leaks. Don't worry, honey; it has a bilge pump and if it begins to leak, we will just turn the pump on and all the water will be sucked out of the boat." It sounded reasonable to me, at the time!

Just for your information; never believe a man who starts a sentence with the words "I think."

We got out into the middle of the lake and as I looked down, there was water sloshing around my feet – not a good sign. Not only was the boat leaking, but he said everything is OK because

Check for Leaks Before You Put a Boat into the Water

he will just turn the bilge pump on. He flipped the switch and, you guessed it, nothing!! The bilge pump didn't work!

When he noticed the terror in my eyes with the thought of going down with the ship and having to swim for it in alligator-infested waters in the dead of winter; my husband suggested that I take over the helm of this leaky vessel. He would wait until I reached a certain speed and then pull the plug and let all of the water run out. Again, it sounded reasonable to me, at the time. Let me think, what should I do? Swim or drive the boat really fast in the direction of the dock? What would you do? I told him "sure, I'd be glad to drive!"

This decision meant that he would stick his head down by the motor, which left another part of his body exposed to God and anyone with binoculars. Let's just say the moon was shining during the day. And by the way, it was a little windy that day; so there were waves.

I learned very quickly that when a man's head is down by the motor, it is hard to hear what he is saying from inside that little hole.

As I was driving toward the dock, it kept getting rougher and rougher and he was flopping around back there like a fish out of water (excuse the pun). I promise that I thought he kept saying to speed up, which I thought meant the boat would eventually even out and drive smoother. I continued to go faster. And just to let you know, I didn't want to slow down and let the boat fill up with more water (which meant the swimming to shore option.)

The faster I went, the more he screamed and flopped around. Are you getting the picture? A storm was also brewing and the waves had picked up.

By this time, I imagined all of our neighbors now knew beyond a shadow of a doubt that if they could just grab their video cameras and get this on video, they could have sent it into the funny videos show and would surely have been ten thousand dollars richer. I wish someone would have done that so they would have shared the money with us and we would have bought a newer boat. Now there is a thought!

I found out that the faster I went, the more the boat jumped the waves and the more pain I was causing my husband with his head stuck down by the motor. After much screaming, I finally figured out that he was saying something about tilting the motor up or down. By this time, the only thing still in the water was the motor. The boat was pretty much airborne as I was jumping from wave to wave and having a blast, I might add.

However, by the time we smoothed out and my husband decided to let me live, we had learned a very big lesson in boating.

1. Boats don't get smoother the faster you drive them.
2. Sometimes tilting the motor helps.
3. If your husband weighs more than a few pounds, you don't want his weight at the back of a sinking boat.
4. Have an escape plan before the boat begins to sink.
5. Don't believe a man who begins a sentence with "I think."

Sometimes there are things in our lives that look all right at first glance, but once they are put to the test in deep water (spiritually speaking), we find out there are leaks in our Christianity.

How many of us have developed spiritual leaks? They just started out small and insignificant but then when we got into deep, rough waters, we found out real fast, the amount of damage that can be done, by one small leak.

What kind of holes do we allow in our everyday lives, that when left unchecked, could become major events?

I pray that as you read this, God reveals to you what that "small leak" is in your life so He can repair it before it begins to grow and then endangers the very ones you love the most.

What leaks in your house?

> One day Jesus said to his disciples, "let's go over to the other side of the lake." So they got into a boat and set out. As they sailed, He fell asleep. A squall came down on the lake, so that the boat was being swamped, and they were in great danger. The disciples went and woke Him, saying, "Master, Master, we're going to drown!" He got up and rebuked the wind and the raging waters; the storm subsided and all was calm. "Where is your faith?" he asked His disciples. In fear and amazement they asked one another, "Who is this? He commands even the winds and the waters, and they obey Him." (Luke 8:22-25 NIV).

Chapter 2

Are You Listening?

I BELIEVE WE need to learn continuously. Almost every day; even in the simplest of situations - God is teaching us.

The question is: are we teachable? I am thankful to say that in my many years of ministry, I have only met a few people who I felt were unteachable. They did not have a learning disability; they had a spiritual disability.

They chose to live in their own world of deception, and we will continue to hold them up in our prayers until their eyes are opened. You cannot teach someone who already knows everything – or should I say, who think they know everything.

We still pray that one day, just as Nebuchadnezzar came to himself, these people will also see the light and become teachable. (No, they didn't eat grass or let their hair grow like feathers.)

Please understand that their deception had nothing to do with doctrine but everything to do with justifying sin. I choose not to argue doctrine; I love and respect other Christians and pray that others would do the same for me.

The Lord is forever teaching, but are we truly listening? Time and time again in His Word, He declares, "He who has an ear, let him hear." (Revelation 2:7 KJV).

How often do we speak to someone, and although the person hears us, they really are not listening? Too often people are thinking about what they will say in return, and therefore miss most of the conversation.

Maybe others are distracted by life and circumstances that have dulled their hearing. I choose sometimes to remain quiet in various situations so that when I do speak, I can be heard. As a youth pastor and minister of music, I am always surrounded by people who are all talking at once or tuning their instruments. It is definitely a challenge to speak and be heard.

When my girls were young, I could ask them to do something for me only to come back later and discover they had not moved. Oh, they heard my voice, but they didn't heed my voice. Normally, I would just eliminate their distraction (such as the phone, computer, or TV.) Eliminating the distraction would achieve the desired result of making them listen to me. It is amazing how well children listen when all the distractions have been removed. How well can we listen when the distractions are removed?

I also have learned the importance of listening for the voice that needs me. As a mother, I could pick out my child's voice from the voices of all the other children playing in the area. If my child was hurt, that sensitivity to the sound of her voice was intensified and I was keen to hear the cry for help from my child above all the other noises that occurred during playtime.

I pray the Lord helps me always to have an ear to hear His voice and a heart to learn.

There have been times when I have been distracted and didn't hear exactly what the Lord was trying to say to me. That's not a good place to be. We need to learn to keep our mouths shut and learn to listen to what God would like to say.

Remember that sometimes God whispers, and sometimes He thunders. I prefer Him to whisper to me, because when I haven't been a good listener, the Lord has thundered - "What are you doing here, Donna?"

I am reminded of the old song about "sweet potato pie and shut my mouth." I have learned that I hear so much more clearly when I learn to keep my mouth shut.

> And the sheep listen to His voice (John 10:3, NIV)

> The Lord said, "go out and stand on the mountain in the presence of the Lord, for the Lord is about to pass by." Then a great and powerful wind tore the mountains apart and shattered the rocks before the Lord, but the Lord was not in the wind. After the wind there was an earthquake, but the Lord was not in the earthquake. After the earthquake came a fire; but the Lord was not in the fire. And after the fire came a gentle whisper. When Elijah heard it, he pulled his cloak over his face and went out and stood at the mouth of the cave. Then a voice said to him, "What are you doing here, Elijah?" (1 Kings 19:11-13, NIV)

Chapter 3

Hidden Snakes

IF YOU SPEAK to anyone who has lived in Florida recently, inevitably the subject of storms (i.e. hurricanes) comes up. I am one of very few Florida-born natives. My dad was a preacher and in the organization we were affiliated with, ministers were pretty much required to move every two years.

I was born in Florida and raised throughout the United States, and I do mean throughout. Only as an adult can I appreciate the education in various cultures I was exposed to as a child.

I have enjoyed and endured the feet of snow that accumulated during an Oregon winter. I have ice skated on lakes and streams in the hills of Pennsylvania. I have witnessed and traveled through some of the worse tornado weather that Kansas and the Midwest has to offer. I have prayed for my stuff not to be washed downstream as what was usually a peaceful creek turned into a raging torrent in less than three hours and washed everything in its path downstream during a flash food in Alabama. We watched 40 foot pine trees float by during this flash flood and thankful they didn't hit our house.

I have driven over the winding roads in the mountains of West Virginia, only to walk across a swinging bridge, to visit people who attended our church and were sick and needed prayer.

It was not until years later, that we experienced the onslaught of hurricanes that brought devastation to Florida as well as other states.

As I previous mentioned, we lived on what was one of the most beautiful lakes in Central Florida. We enjoyed boating, fishing, tubing, swimming, skiing and just sitting by the lake on those rare occasions when we actually had time off. Before the hurricanes, there was approximately six feet of air between our dock and the water.

Following the four or five hurricanes in a row, our dock was two feet under water, and stayed that way for close to two years. What used to be a pretty, sandy beach was grassy and flooded up into our yard and into what had been a nice boathouse we used for storage. Okay, so it was a shed, but we liked to call it a boathouse. By faith, it was a boathouse! The lake had swallowed up approximately thirty feet of yard and some of our shed, oops I mean boathouse.

We always understood that living on a lake does have its drawbacks. We were just so thankful that we did not blow away during the hurricanes that the shed – oops, sorry, boathouse – was the least of our worries. It lost its roof and was a little flooded, but that had happened in August and now it was Christmas time.

At the time of the hurricanes, we prayed for the Lord to watch over our home, we forgot to mention the shed. Now there may be those people who store everything in air-proof, bomb-proof containers, but as I mentioned, we were on a tight budget. Time and money was not something we had a lot of, so if something got in a plastic container, we attempted to secure the lids the best we could. However, every teenager in our church had needed to get something out of that shed and things were definitely not left in order following the floods.

It was now time to put up Christmas decorations. The fact that it was nighttime and cold made no difference. I convinced my husband to go to the shed and look for our Christmas decorations and at least look for the ones that actually made it through the storm. We had not done anything to the shed except make the necessary roof repairs and throw the obviously destroyed items away. It didn't even have a door.

My husband, being the wise man of God he is, said he would go get the stuff but only if I went with him to hold the light. I don't like spiders and bugs and I didn't want to trek to the shed at night when the creatures of the night might decide they liked me – a lot!

Thank God this trip went without incident – or should I say "not a creature was stirring, not even a mouse." When we got to the shed, we did a snatch and grab and made a run for it. I just knew there was a spider setting the table to have me for supper.

The next day, my man began the arduous task of deep cleaning the shed. He was throwing things away that got ruined during the wind, rain and flooding of the hurricanes. While he was there, he spotted a small, two-foot-long moccasin and I don't mean something you wear on your feet.

For those who do not believe you should ever kill anything, please skip to the next chapter. Moccasins are known for having a bad attitude when cornered, or maybe they are just born to be like that person you know, whose name you never mention out loud, but we all know who they are with bad attitudes.

This very tiny snake with a King Kong attitude began to jump, strike and basically show its long, ugly tail. My husband quickly sent him to where snakes go when they die and was very proud of his accomplishment. Please remember that we had been in the same shed the night before searching for Christmas decorations.

As he went back to cleaning out the shed, he began to clean out one of those big plastic bins that should have held our Christmas stuff. When he reached the bottom of the bin, he removed a basket and found the small snake's momma.

Just to remind you, these snakes are known for their attitude when cornered, and they would much rather fight than flee. When he had collected himself, he found that the snake had never moved, you would have thought it was dead. But it was very much alive.

In the meantime, he went to retrieve a chair. Yes, my brave, strong, very healthy husband decided to get a chair to stand on for the task of removing this snake. You didn't think he and the snake would remain on the same level did you? I know there's a sermon in that statement somewhere.

As he again regained himself, he removed the snake. Yes, he did find out just how large and alive it was when he began to relocate it. We believe that not only could God close the mouths of lions for Daniel, but he also closed the mouth of a snake for my man.

How many of us have faced the storms and come through victorious, only to find out that months down the road; the storms blew in something so unexpected, yet so deadly?

How often has God protected us but we were unaware that the danger was even there? Has an unexpected storm blown in unexpected trials? My God is able to calm the storms in our life, and he can shut the mouth of the enemy.

No, we don't profess to be snake handlers, but we do believe that if the need arises, we have a God great enough to take care of the problem. We believe that, according to the Word of God, we can pray for the sick and they will recover, but you can rest assured, I don't go around picking up every snake I come across just to test God.

What has been hidden since your last storm?

> They shall take up serpents; and if they drink any deadly thing, it shall not hurt them; they shall lay hands on the sick, and they shall recover. (Mark 16:18 KJV).

Chapter 4

Never Push a Drowning Victim into the Deep

Just Trying to Help

HAVE YOU EVER met someone who was sincerely trying to help but in reality was no help at all? And after this person's help, you felt worse about the situation?

I have a dear friend – the most precious woman in the world – who had a family member who was bound to a wheelchair because of a tragic accident that left him paralyzed. One day when they were out and about, she was attempting to help her physically challenged husband into the car, and a very nice gentleman saw this and wanted to help.

He helped and then inadvertently closed the door on one of the gentleman's legs, breaking his leg.

What this good helpful gentleman thought was her struggling to get her husband into the car was actually her attempting to handle him correctly so she would not injure either of them in the transfer from wheelchair to the car.

She was grateful that someone wanted to help her, but in reality, the help ended up hurting more than it helped. We need to be sensitive to those we want to help.

A similar situation happened to us while we were on a youth trip. As youth pastors, we take our youth on regular yearly trips. It gives them something to look forward to and united them as a youth group. Not all of our trips are spiritual and not all of our trips are just for fun. There must be a balance.

The Ichetucknee State Park near White Springs in North Florida is a wonderful way to spend the day. When we go, we always take a picnic lunch and let the youth tube down the beautiful crystal-clear, freezing cold, spring-fed river.

The first thing to remember if someone is drowning is to never push them into the deep water. Sounds kind of simple, doesn't it?

Sometimes what we think is the best thing for someone could be the very thing that sends them over the edge (i.e., into the deep.) Have you ever met a person who had good intentions but a bad plan? A bad plan with good intentions can hurt somebody!

There are several ways to enter the river and get on your tube. If you enter at the mid-point you can put in and tube for approximately one hour and then get on a tram that takes you back to the mid-point to do it again and again. There are longer runs, but we have found that this one does best for our youth so they are not stuck in the water for long periods of time.

We try not to think about what happens to those who have to go (you know, go!) during a much longer run. Lots of teens, lots of Cokes, small bladders - Anyway, you get the picture.

There are two ways to get into the river at midpoint – the easy way and the fun way. Well, as you guessed it, we always put in the fun way. The easy way is to walk approximately twenty-five yards upstream; place your tube at the edge of the water where the current is calm, and slowly proceed to the center of the river, where a smooth current will leisurely carry you and your tube down the river.

Then there is the "fun" way, which is to walk onto a floating dock that extends into the fast current of the river and attempt to jump on your tube before it is swept downstream without you. This is always a great photo opportunity while we watch the youth and chaperones attempt to get on their tubes. I do strongly stress the word attempt.

It's a pretty simple approach:

1. Place tube in water.
2. Jump on tube before it leaves without you.

However, truth be told, if you actually land on the tube, it has a tendency to flip you off the other side. (Great photo moment number one as the tube so rudely tosses them on their heads.) No matter what you have been taught about gravity, when entering the stream, it's bottoms up as they flip into the ice-cold water and their tubes proudly proceed without them. They always come up screaming and spitting and chasing their tubes.

(Great photo moment number two or a blackmail moment, whatever you may be into.)

For many years, I had successfully accomplished the task of jumping onto my tube. Most of the time, I successfully held on without getting bucked into the water. There were a few times when I was not successful and someone else had a great photo moment number three which included me falling into the ice-cold water. I would swim to my tube, laugh off all the jokes and proceed to have a great day with nothing ever affected but my pride. I would simply proceed to catch my tube and try the arduous task of picking my backside up out of the ice-cold water. Most times, I couldn't feel my backside. I don't understand how picking up something you can't even feel should be so hard. And that's all I'm gonna say about that.

Well for some reason, this trip was not going to be anything like the previous ones. After taking all of my photos of everyone else, I secured my camera, secured my bathing suit, and convinced myself that the only thing that would freeze would be my large bottom side, which pokes precariously through the bottom of the tube when you sit on it. However, my tube had different motives. I truly believe I had rented a defective or possessed tube. Can tubes be possessed? I think this one was.

As I jumped on the tube, it so rudely flipped me off like, I had just gotten on the world's meanest bull. It was an instant on, instant off, kind of bull/tube ride. I never even fully got out of the chute.

As I entered the water, I held what little breath I could (having asthma) and popped up quite quickly, but for some reason, my lungs decided the water was a little bit too cold to operate, so they just shut down.

No air, Boom! No air! Everyone watching was getting their laughs in as I struggled to find my tube or swim upstream back to the dock, which was getting out of my reach much faster than I needed it to. I knew if I could just reach the dock before passing out, I would live.

However, my husband, after viewing the whole incident, decided that I had just fallen in and swallowed half the river and would be fine, as always. Not the case! With all of my strength, I swam toward the dock and was two feet from grabbing the dock when my beloved husband of twenty-five-plus years decided he would "help" me to my tube, which was somewhere far downstream and in the middle of the current.

As I reached with all the breath I had left in me to grab the dock, my husband grabbed me and threw me into the deep toward what he thought was my tube. If I'd had life insurance, I would have sworn he wanted to collect it and had finally found his opportunity to never listen to my backseat driving again. He has always said that those things don't bother him, but in a split second I knew it did!

Of course, there was no tube, there was still no air and there were other tubers coming downstream with their family and friends watching this half-crazed old lady trying to breathe. I think they just thought I was panicking, which by now I was. It is a miracle I didn't pass out.

I was attempting to swim and breathe all the while praying that God would let me live and breathe again.

By this time, one of our adult chaperones, threw me a tube, and I managed to hold on to it long enough to catch a little air as he began to swim me back to the dock (upstream).

Just for your information, he later married one of my daughters. If you ever want to impress the parents, just save one of them from drowning; believe me, it works.

Well my future son-in-law finally pulled me safely back to the dock. I was able to take some asthma meds, which eventually stopped the attack. It is only by the grace of God that my lungs did not close up totally (which has happened to people I loved dearly – and their outcome was tragically different).

After taking my meds and catching my breath, I explained to my husband about the asthma attached and he felt so bad that he didn't notice and had thrown me into the deep.

By no means am I telling you to handle your illness in the same way I handled my scary encounter with the tube. However, I do know when the enemy is attacking me. The devil wants me to live in fear and to live in my sickness. I refuse to do anything the devil wants me to do.

I was and am still today – determined to not give into fear. I decided to get back into the river, but this time, I gently got on my tube from the shore and proceeded downstream. Breathing is something we take for granted until it is not there. I was very thankful to be able to breathe again.

Again, to make a point, a lot of times what we think is wrong with someone really isn't the problem. If we're not careful we will cause others more harm than good by not being sensitive to what is truly wrong with them. Spiritually speaking; it could cost them their spiritual breath or maybe even their spiritual life.

I never want to assume I have all the answers, and I never want to push someone further into the deep when they are just about to reach a spiritual breakthrough.

I have seen this happen so many times in the lives of our youth. Well-meaning adults who thought they knew what was best for them ended up pushing them away instead of wrapping their arms around them and pulling them into the loving arms of safety – which is Jesus Christ. Teens would get discouraged and walk away from the faith when they were actually on the brink of giving their lives over to Jesus.

To this day, there are some who never made it back into their spiritual dock. I keep praying they will and I've come to the point where I tell well-meaning Christian friends to never assume they know what is best. Good intention – bad plan!

Please remember to be kind with your words. Be loving, be encouraging, and be very careful never to send people into the rushing water of the enemy, thinking they are strong enough to swim. We need to throw them spiritual floats with our words and deeds instead of just assuming they have the air to swim.

It's not that they can't swim; they could just be out of air. The battles of this life may have already taken all the air they have and one more battle will send them under.

As I write this, I am compelled to tell you that no matter what kind of dirty looks you get or what people may think, when you need to get to shore, tell someone.

There is always someone who will pray, someone who will toss you a life jacket and throw his or her arms around you to help you swim upstream into the safe and loving arms of our Lord and Savior Jesus Christ.

He is waiting at the dock to heal you, to love you and to help you get back into the stream of life. If you need prayer and the raging water has become too swift, find a prayer warrior who will pray and encourage you.

Oh by the way, I forgave my husband who really felt bad when he found out I was having a full blown asthma attack. We are still happily married, but I tell him all the time that I will never let him live it down. I'm sure he will do something else and it will make a great chapter in my next book. Bottom line, I still love making memories with him and would not change a thing.

I'm reminded of an old song I learned when I was a teenager and would visit a Baptist church youth group in Alabama.

When I think I'm going under Part the Waters Lord
When I feel the waves around me calm the sea

When I cry for help oh hear me Lord and hold out Your hand
Touch my life – still the raging storm in me.

> "Lord, if it's you," Peter replied, "tell me to come to you on the water." "Come," He said. Then Peter got down out of the boat, walked on the water and came toward Jesus. But when he saw the wind, he was afraid and beginning to sink, cried out, "Lord, save me!" Immediately Jesus reached out his hand and caught him. "You of little faith," He said, "why did you doubt?" And when they climbed into the boat, the wind died down. (Matthew 14:28-32 NIV)

Chapter 5

Missing Ingredients

I CONFESS THAT I am a social eater. I can eat for any reason. If there isn't an occasion, I eat anyway. I eat when I'm happy and I eat when I'm sad.

There isn't a better time to socialize than after church on a Sunday evening. It used to be the social event of the week. We would gather in (or take over) a small restaurant in this small town and spend the rest of the evening laughing, talking and of course eating.

Because it's a small town, there are few choices on places to eat. This month's preferred choice was pizza. We were waited on by the only waitress in the place, who needed a course in tableside manners. We waited for what seemed to be hours for our food to arrive.

Just because I think it needs mentioning, we over-tip all servers. Whether they are pleasant, rude, quick, or slow, we always over-tip. It is not that we have extra money to waste, but we believe Christians should be the nicest people to be served and leave the biggest tips. You never know what a server may be going through in their personal lives. In addition, the server is not the cook – so no need to blame them.

However, we frequently go out to eat with fellow Christians who are rude, demanding and leave horrible tips, if they leave any at all. We have been known to leave a tip in their place after they leave the table.

Again, we live in a small town, and hopefully, one day these servers may be touched by a kind word or an unexpected tip. Doesn't everybody need the Lord?

Back to my subject. We are determined to make the best of every situation, so slow service just means more stories and time to spend with people we love. Most of the time, this theory works, but there are extreme occasions when a server is determined to make everyone as miserable as he or she is and this was one of those times.

This night we were served pizza with no sauce! Pizza without sauce is like eating saltine crackers without anything to drink. Just picture this; thick crust, pepperoni, and melted cheese. No sauce! It just isn't pizza without all the ingredients.

Neither is a Christian a Christ-like person without all the ingredients. What good are Christians if they have everything but love? They are not good for anything according to I Corinthians 13.

Pizza without sauce is like a Christian without love. Love should be the main ingredient in our Christian lives. How can we call ourselves Christians when we're missing the main ingredient? Just spend a little time with people and you'll find out real fast if their pizza is missing sauce or is just short a few slices of pepperoni.

Be cheerful no matter what; pray all the time; thank God no matter what happens. This is the way God wants you who belong to Christ Jesus to live. (1 Thessalonians 5:16-18 MSG).

Giving thanks always for all things to God the Father in the name of our Lord Jesus Christ. (Ephesians 5:30 NKJV)

A gentle answer turns away wrath, but a harsh word stirs up anger. (Proverbs 15:1 NIV)

Chapter 6

Shipwrecked on Dry Ground

MY NEPHEW WAS attending a Christian College out of state so his father decided that driving an 18-wheeler, cross-country could earn him the funds needed to help his son stay in college.

It was a beautiful, sunny day in Florida and I had gone with my sister-in-law to see my brother off, which I had done numerous times. However, for some reason, I was very uneasy about this trip. I kept it to myself, but later I learned it was the Lord trying to get my attention, if for no other reason than to pray.

On this trip, my brother was pulling a flatbed trailer with two other flatbed trailers piggybacking on top of each other.

The next afternoon, I was visiting my mom when we got a call that there had been an accident in Louisiana and my brother was injured. They would not tell us much except we should get there right away.

This news was followed by close friends making quick decisions. Relatives had recently won some money and had given some of their winning to my mom. It was the exact amount we needed for a couple of airline tickets. I believe God uses strange methods to supply for His children, and my sister-in-law and I rushed to the airport to fly to Louisiana. There also were numerous friends who went far and beyond to help us get to my brother.

We were both unsure of what to do when we got there, but we had thought we would just rent a vehicle to get us from the airport to Sulfur, Louisiana (approximately a two-hour drive from the airport.) We knew he had internal injuries but we were not sure of their severity.

We learned on the flight that he had not wrecked his truck. He had pulled well off the road and was redoing a strap on his load that had come loose. As he walked around the back of the trailer, a woman lost control of her car and slid into him and the truck. We later were saddened to learn that the wreck killed her instantly. We held her family up in prayer.

We were relieved that my brother had not wrecked his truck or fallen asleep and gone off an overpass or over an embankment. However, the thought of a car going between 60 and 70 mph hitting him brought a sickness to the pit of my stomach unlike I had ever felt before.

The plane ride was turbulent, yet that was not what was making me sick. In our wildest imaginations, we could not picture what lay ahead. We had thoughts of whether he would even be alive by the time we got there, but we quickly set those thoughts aside and prayed.

During a very short layover in Texas, we attempted to rent a car from the airport. We were rudely turned away because we didn't have a credit card.

For years, our families had been adamant about paying off all of our credit cards and getting out of debt which we had both done. We felt like we had accomplished a great deal by paying off our credit cards and not possessing any card so it would not tempt us into going back into debt. We had heard preachers teaching for years to "get out of debt"... so we did. We never thought an emergency might arise when just one card would have come in handy.

I even got desperate enough to call a local pastor from our denomination. As you may have guessed, he was just about as rude as the rental car agent. I understand there are a lot of people out there who take advantage of pastors. I however suggest that pastors don't just throw everyone into the same category and do some homework before they write everyone off. There are people out there who are legit and sometimes end up in a desperate situation.

We finally got back on the plane, defeated because we knew the same fate awaited us in Louisiana and we would be unable to continue to the hospital without a rental car.

I had seen in the movies where people seem to get very close to each other on airplanes, so we decided to share our dilemma with the flight attendant. She made an announcement to the other passengers to see if anyone was going to Sulfur and would mind two tagalongs. We were thankful to hear that a woman had volunteered. She asked us many questions to set to rest her fear that we were Thelma and Louise wannabees.

She was such a lovely, sweet lady, and we hit it off from the moment we met her. We knew God had everything under control even though we didn't seem to have anything under control.

After the plane landed in Louisiana and we were leaving the plane, we saw another woman holding a sign with our names on it. While we were in transit, calls had been made, contacts were set up and friends from Florida had spoken to friends from Louisiana and arranged our transportation.

Again I say, isn't it great how God has everything under control? The fact of the matter is, we really didn't have anything to do with it. God was working behind the scenes even before our arrival. What a great God we serve!

We thanked the gracious Good Samaritan that we had met on the plane and proceeded to be transported by a new gracious stranger.

She took us to her home, fed us a snack and drove the two hours from the airport to Sulfur. She took a short nap at the hospital and then turned right around and went back home.

She would not allow us to give her any money for gas or anything else. I do believe that to this day, God is blessing her and her family just because of this one kind deed.

Isn't it amazing how, when you think God has truly left you stranded, you realize he has been there all along working behind the scenes?

We finally arrived at the hospital and it was hard to recognize my brother through all of the blood, swelling, bruises, scrapes, cuts, holes, etc. In addition, they had him hooked up to life support, which was breathing for him.

The ICU staff was very helpful and gracious to our family the entire time he was in ICU. (Which was about six weeks.)

We prayed, and he fought hard. I would love to say that we just scooped him up with all our faith and took him home, and everything was a miracle. The fact of the matter; is sometimes miracles are sudden and sometimes they are a process.

Another fact is, there were a few years of surgeries, including screws and bolts holding things back together. Doctors told us he would never walk and there also were times he battled depression before he was able to proceed with any semblance of life as he once knew it. My brother surviving the accident was a miracle all by itself.

Not only was he able to walk again, now he is a senior pastor at a church in Florida. He works out and plays racquetball at least two times a week, which just confirms that miraculous sustaining power of God.

When our world comes crashing down, God is there to pick up the pieces and put us back together so we can accomplish what He has called us to do. What a realization of the Scripture, "He will never leave you nor forsake you," even when you think He has.

> And be content with such things as you have; for he hath said, "I will never leave thee, nor forsake thee." (Hebrews 13:5 KJV)

Chapter 7

Opossums and Pontiacs

SMELLS ARE VERY important to most women. If they weren't then why would we bathe with perfumed soap, wash our hair in something equally as nice and cover ourselves with fine perfume before leaving a house that has the smell of freshly extinguished season candles?

All of that to say that smells are so important that I will purchase a pastry at the grocery store when I'm not even hungry. I can pass a pizza shop in the mall and suddenly crave pizza. Just as quickly, I can pass a road kill and suddenly I've lost my appetite. So you can only imagine how embarrassed I was when suddenly I was hit with a smelly situation.

I was on my way to a church convention in my freshly washed car that we called The Bonnie. I was dressed in my best clothes, freshly cut hair and of course a new manicure.

Most of the year, my car is full of toys and sticky with tiny little fingerprints all over the glass from where my grandchildren were trying to paint slobber pictures on the windows. Now you know the real me; don't judge!

I digress. There are people at the convention that I only see once a year, and we love to catch up on old times and do lots of fellowshipping. Fellowshipping is a churchy term for eating. Church people can fellowship on any occasion, for any reason and at any time.

Being in ministry, my husband and I like to make a good impression on everyone we meet. My man had purchased an old Pontiac after we totaled a van we were driving. That will have to be in another chapter.

We were told that The Bonnie was owned by a sweet little old lady who only drove it to church and the grocery store. We believed them, and that's all I'm gonna say about that.

This wasn't a new Pontiac, but it got us from point A to point B most of the time. I never thought much about what I drove until it was convention time and I saw what everyone else was driving. It seemed to me that we were the only ones not driving an expensive new vehicle. Talk about intimidation.

> Note to self – write a chapter on how we should never compare ourselves to others and just be all that God created us to be.

I had allowed the enemy (the devil) to convince me that God loved everybody else at the convention more than He loved me. I could picture a huge spotlight shining on us and The Bonnie as we drove into the parking lot with a loudspeaker informing everyone at the convention "The Smith family lacks faith; just see what they are driving?" Did I mention that I have a wild imagination?

The drive to the convention was forty five minutes through the beautiful outback of Florida. No towns, no gas stations, nothing but wide-open spaces.

On my way to the convention, I hit one of the largest opossums I had ever laid eyes on. It looked about the size of a small elephant to me, but who am I to judge? It was at least five feet tall and weighted in excess of three hundred pounds. As least that's the way I saw it right before I creamed it with The Bonnie.

Anyway, I was hoping he would duck, but instead just about the time I tried to straddle him he decided to take another peek at my car. Sometimes you just need to learn how to duck! Maybe he was having a bad day, or maybe he was just being too nosey. Aren't opossums supposed to play dead when they get frightened? Well this one must have failed playing dead 101, but I can promise you, he passed the class real fast.

The sound of me hitting this creature was much more than my stomach could take. You would think this was bad enough, sending a poor, defenseless animal to the great animal kingdom in the sky, but things got worse.

As soon as I got home, I told my man that I had hit this huge opossum and I didn't think all of him made it out from under my car. My husband got the water hose and cleaned my car off the best that he could, or at least that's the story he told me and I believed him. It's not good to assume, but I assumed it was all taken care of.

The next day, I got up and drove the forty five minutes back to the convention, parked in my usual spot next to all the new vehicles and proceeded to spend the best part of the morning at the convention. When it was time to go for lunch, I went outside and could smell the car long before I saw it. The opossum, or what was left of him, was still under my car.

I was mortified, and when I got home, my man was back out under the car doing all he could to remove the smelly remnants of the opossum.

Again, I got up early, the next day, and returned to the convention. Then when it came time to eat and that hot summer Florida sun began to do its thing – yes, you guessed it. More cooked opossum. Please note that I could not use the air conditioner during this time or the smell would permeate the inside of The Bonnie as bad as it was on the outside. Also, you can only imagine what driving in 100 percent humidity with the windows down can do to a hairdo. Don't leave you windows down in 100 percent humidity and then complain when your hair frizzes!

By the time this had happened for a couple of days, I began to park way out in the middle of a field with hopes that no one would want to walk that far so no one could smell my car.

I heard that in the old days that people would eat these notorious creatures, but I promise you, I would never eat anything that smelled that bad.

You think that finally, I would have learned my lesson and my husband would have gotten the remnants of this elusive creature out from under my car but it never happened.

It was weeks before the smell finally dissipated and we were able to drive without the windows down and use the air conditioning without the fresh smell of rotten opossum.

I did learn something from this experience. Now that you know what stinks around my house when things heat up, I ask you the same question. What stinks at your house when things heat up? What smelly remains are we still carrying around with us regarding something that we should have let die years ago? We just carry around the remains, hoping no one will notice the awful stench.

I pray that our everyday lives will be a sweet smell to everyone we come in contact with. What kind of a smell are you leaving for people to remember you by? Just like you can smell great perfume in a room after someone has walked through, I pray that we leave a beautiful Christ-like fragrance everywhere we go and to everyone we meet. It doesn't take a lot of effort.

> In the Messiah, in Christ, God leads us from place to place in one perpetual victory parade. Through us, he brings knowledge of Christ. Everywhere we go, people breathe in the exquisite fragrance. Because of Christ, we give off a sweet scent arising to God, which is recognized by those on the way of salvation – an aroma redolent with life... (2 Corinthians 2:14-16 MSG).

Chapter 8

A Dog Named Budweiser

HOW COULD ANYTHING good come from a dog named Budweiser?

Following thirty years of ministry, my dad was forced to take an early retirement due to Parkinson's disease. Although he was blessed to not shake much, the disease robbed him of his beautiful baritone, preacher-man voice.

I've heard the statement many times about preachers who may not be paid well, but the retirement plan is eternal. This plan is great when we get to Heaven, but he had to take an early earthly retirement. They were not prepared or financially able to do so, but due to the loss of voice and difficulty of speech and limited mobility, it was necessary.

They were forced to move into a small three-bedroom mobile home with us until we could afford something larger, so we were elated when we finally found "the big house" in a great neighborhood, and the house actually came with a mother-in-law suite.

It was like the house was made just for us. The previous owners had twins and in-laws, just like we did. We will always love that home and have fond memories of the time we spent there.

The house came with a swimming pool and a nice neighborhood. My dad could swim and ride his bike to keep his health as good as possible. If he wasn't swimming (year round; it was in Florida), he would bike daily just for exercise.

The home was located one block from the intra-coastal waterway. My dad loved to pastor, and he loved to fish. Now that he couldn't pastor, he could still fish. He would walk to the park to fish or ride his bike, whatever he felt like doing that day.

When we moved into the neighborhood, our children quickly met and played with all the other children in the area, which consisted of other sets of twins. There also was a neighborhood dog named none other than Budweiser.

An elderly couple just a few houses down owned this beautiful, huge, fat black Labrador retriever that they treated like one of their children. They would let him out in the mornings to play with all the other children and would get in their car in the evenings and go pick him up after a long day of him entertaining the neighborhood children.

The dog was very intimidating when we first saw him, and we wondered if he was safe, but when we saw how he played with all the other kids on the block, we realized, along with the other neighbors, that this was just that – a neighborhood dog.

My dad was an old-fashioned man of God and he wanted nothing to do with a dog named after the king of beers. He didn't even like it when the girls talked about playing with Budweiser all day. However, every morning when he got up early to get in some good fishing, Budweiser would follow him to the park and play while my dad fished and then follow him all the way back home.

Every morning it was the same thing. He would try to get Budweiser to leave him alone. "Go home Budweiser!" But just like that, Budweiser would pay no attention to my dad's commands and follow him to and from the park just like he was his dog.

My dad complained daily about that stupid dog following him around. He didn't want people to think that the king of beers dog belonged to the retired preacher man. That just wouldn't look holy I guess.

One morning my dad got his fishing pole, loaded up on his bike and made his trek to the park to do some early morning fishing. As usual, Budweiser was right on his heels. However, this would not be the usual fishing trip.

After fishing for a few minutes, my dad noticed a car circle the park a couple of times before stopping. Out jumped a group of young men making a beeline for my dad. As he turned, he knew they were only there to rob him or worse. As they began running toward him, Budweiser jumped between them and my dad to let them know that they were not coming any closer without the fight of their life.

Never in all the time we had known the dog, with kids jumping on him, pulling his tail and loving everybody in the neighborhood, had he ever shown any sign of aggression whatsoever. But on this day, he sounded like a pack of dogs all wrapped into one sleek, fat, black, glossy ball of fur standing straight up on Budweiser's back. Dogs definitely have a sixth sense.

The gang quickly returned to the car, where they sped away without ever looking back. Not only had Budweiser saved my dad's life, but he had also held off an entire gang of young men.

I believe you know the rest of the story. Never did I hear my dad complain again about Budweiser following him anywhere.

We could even hear my dad calling Budweiser on his early-morning fishing trips. He found out the hard way that God can even use a dog named Budweiser if He needs to.

Every now and then we visit the old neighborhood for a "used-to" tour. We used to live here, we used to play there, etc. and of course, we always reminisce about the neighborhood dog that saved my dad's life.

The king of all creation used the king of beers dog for a miracle early one hot Florida morning. I never did remember if Dad said whether he caught anything that day.

> So do not fear, for I am with you; do not be dismayed, for I am your God. I will strengthen you and help you; I will uphold you with my righteous right hand (Isaiah 41:10)

Chapter 9

Cooks and Christians

AS I MENTIONED before, we love to eat and have some of the strangest experiences in life just trying to get a good meal.

I don't know why we are so hard headed that we didn't think that maybe God just wanted us to fast or just eat at home.

After a great Sunday evening service with a guest evangelist, we decided to take the evangelist out to eat. After all, he had definitely worked up a great appetite. We picked a restaurant where we could eat and feel free to visit because this restaurant was open all night.

After waiting for over an hour to just get the basics, such as water, a menu, and drinks; then actually someone to take our order, we heard a commotion at the front door. There was a knife-wielding man in a blood-stained apron screaming in a language other than English and waving this huge knife around. I'm sure he was swearing at the manager, but we didn't know whether to laugh or dive under the tables.

He screamed and waved his knife and then promptly left the restaurant. Now of course this was a great humorous, one-liner time for all of our friends. Come to find out, what we were joking about really was happening. He was the cook and he quit.

It wasn't so much that he quit or just how he quit, but he quit because we had come into the restaurant to eat.

Now please correct me if I'm wrong, but isn't that what restaurants are for – eating? I still could be wrong, but if you're hired as a cook at a restaurant, wouldn't you just assume that you would eventually have to cook something? The waitress informed us that the cook got mad that we had come in and promptly quit. Well we didn't want any more knife-wielding cooks flying out of restaurants, so we just decided to go eat pizza.

Spiritually speaking; how many times do unsaved people come into our church looking for something good to eat, only to find out that the cook has quit? There is no one to wait on them, and there are no servers with table etiquette.

I believe our churches need to be more patron friendly. The Lord is sending us people who are hurting and hungry. Their bread/life is dry, and they need a good meal, only to find out we're serving stale bread in the House of Bread. What is wrong with this picture?

I believe that just as fresh bread smells good for miles around, the fresh bread of the anointing should smell for miles around. People throughout not only the neighborhood but also the town should know that our church is a place to receive a good spiritual meal.

The best spiritual meals in town should be served at our church. Anyone can read a menu, anyone can open a restaurant, but it doesn't take long for a reputation to get out about a restaurant having great food or making people sick.

Does your church give people spiritual food poisoning? Are they choking on bitterness? Old mind-sets? Or stale bread that should have been thrown away years ago? People come looking for something other than what they have to eat every day of their lives and all we offer them is the same thing they can find on the streets.

Some churches host people who are jealous of other people in the church, people who gossip about other people or who compare bank accounts to see who God has blessed the most. What kind of bread are we serving the world?

I believe it's high time for us to spend more spiritual time in the kitchen so patrons who come into our spiritual restaurant, aren't fed contaminated food, but the fresh bread of the Word of God. This delicious bread should be seasoned with love, salted with caring, peppered with grace, sugared with tenderness and glazed with tons of mercy.

We are not God – we can't change people – but we can invite them to a feast that will change their lives forever. It is like the woman at the well who asked for water and Jesus said, "If you just knew who I was. I will give you water from a well where you will never thirst again."

Are we serving contaminated water? Are we serving contaminated food, or are we preparing a feast for sinners that will change their lives forever to the point that they will never thirst again?

> A woman of Samaria came to draw water, Jesus said to her, "Give Me a drink." For His disciples had gone away into the city to buy food. Then the woman of Samaria said to Him, "How is it that You, being a Jew, ask a drink from me, a Samaritan woman?"

For Jews have no dealings with Samaritans. Jesus answered and said to her, "If you knew the gift of God, and who it is who says to you, "Give Me a drink, you would have asked Him, and He would have given you living water."

The woman said to Him, "Sir, You have nothing to draw with and the well is deep. Where then do You get that living water? Are You greater than our father Jacob, who gave us the well, and drank from it himself, as well as his sons and his livestock?"

Jesus answered and said to her, "Whoever drinks of this water will thirst again, but whoever drinks of the water that I shall give him will never thirst. But the water that I shall give him will become in him a fountain of water springing up into everlasting life."

The woman said to Him, "Sir, give me this water, that I may not thirst, nor come here to draw," (John 4:7-15 NKJV)

Chapter 10

Blood, Bruises and the Bathtub

RAISING TWINS WAS a feat all in itself. Then raising twins with my mother and retired minister dad living in the house with us created issues all their own. Do you remember the old cartoons of the cat and dog when the dog would wait till the very last minute and sneak up on the cat, then bark like crazy? All of this would make the frazzled cat cling to the ceiling. That was our home at that time.

We called it "the cat on the ceiling syndrome." We were people who were easily frazzled. Have you ever met people that when you say hello, they next thing you know, they are hanging from the ceiling and you aren't sure what just happened to set them off?

My mother, bless her heart, could be a cat-on-the ceiling type of mom from time to time. (Not all the time, just from time to time.) It was not because she was just that way, but the pressures of years of ministry had left its mark.

It could have been the stress of retiring early, losing their home; taking care of her husband who was in failing health; being pushed into a home that was not her own; and making the best of what should have been her retirement and her quite years. Now her life was anything but quiet with two small, screaming little girls.

Girls scream/squeal anyway. They're girls, they scream, they squeal, they make noise. When God made girls, He created a tone that no one else on the planet can hit unless you are a girl, and my girls were no exception.

After we had twins and were youth pastors for many years, God helped us come to the conclusion that to truly be a great parent or youth pastor, you must be able to deal with organized chaos. If someone isn't killing somebody, you choose your battles. If nobody's hurt, it will work out. Sometimes it's better to coach than to referee. Coaches can teach and encourage, but it's up to the players on how good they play. A referee is only there to point out the penalties.

I prefer to coach. Penalties are something teens can work out on their own time/with their own parents. Don't have a cow, I know there are penalties for certain infractions, but I have learned it is easier for us to focus the youth into areas where there will not likely be so many infractions.

My twins' pediatrician had told us before they were born that because they were premature, they would be slower than all the other children, they would be sickly and they might never be normal.

After I heard this come from his mouth, I purposed in my heart that they would not be slow, they would not be sickly and they would be as normal as God would allow them to be.

Believe me, God will answer our prayers when we get hard headed about things, and boy did He answer that one.

My girls have been anything but slow. They don't have a slow bone in them, and they were walking at ten and eleven months old. I think they've been talking since the day they were born. They are both very gifted musically and vocally and in teaching ministry.

I had placed both of them in the bathtub one evening to get their baths before supper (dinner for those from the North). I thought they were old enough to do it by themselves, but what I didn't know was they had been watching too much gymnastics on TV and mistook the towel rack for the uneven bars.

While one was keeping watch for mom, the other one decided to try her expertise on the high bar. Unlike the ones seen on TV, our towel rack was not reinforced with high-grade steel or fastened to anything other than drywall. It was only supposed to hold towels. How much reinforcement do you need for hanging towels?

Well of course about the time the youngest one got her feet above her head, the whole towel rack gave way, plunging her into the faucet and slicing a hole in her head. It wouldn't be the first or the last time that another hole was added to her knot head.

As you can only imagine, she was screaming bloody murder with a head wound ejecting blood everywhere. Her twin sister also was screaming because she had witnessed the entire thing and knew that her twin's head had been hurt tremendously by the sound it made when it hit the faucet.

Before my mother and I, who were cooking supper at the time, could get into the bathroom, they came running out. One was screaming because she was hurt and saw blood. The other one was screaming because of what she witness and she also saw blood. Then to top it off, my mother started screaming because she didn't know what had happened and she saw blood. She just saw the blood and assumed the worst.

Please picture me trying to figure out what happened and why, were three females all screaming. I couldn't hear what the girls were trying to tell me because my mom was too busy screaming with them. Later, I really wished I had a video of this event.

Following several attempts on my part to find out who was hurt, how hurt they were, and whether the event needed me to join in the screaming; I finally decided to take control.

Rarely if ever was the term "shut up" used in our home. We always were careful about all words used in front of the girls so we would raise nice young ladies and not little sailors. However, drastic matters call for drastic measures.

I screamed for all of them to "shut up!" This, of course got their attention real quickly considering my own mother also was a part of the chaos.

When my girls heard me tell everyone to shut up, you would have thought I had just blasphemed God Himself. You could have heard a pin drop. Never mind the pain my daughter was in or the distress of the other one who was the witness. I had crossed the invisible line of saying shut up, and it could have included my mom who they called Mamaw.

It is a wonder that the gates of hell did not open up and swallow me whole right there on the spot.

My dad had heard the commotion and was just in time for the silence of the twins. The girls began to tell their story, one at a time and we examined the gash in her head and decided stitches were probably needed. Stiches may have been needed for no other reason than to hold her hard head together.

Other than my daughter being extremely head strong and hard headed, there have been no lasting effects from her gymnastics debut in the bathroom. I have, however, learned that sometimes we can get ourselves in such a state where Jesus just has to tell us to shut up and he will fix it. We're so busy trying to fix it ourselves until all we bring is mass confusion.

There comes a time in our spiritual lives when we just need to stand still, be quiet, and know that He is God and he has a good idea of how everything happened. He just wanted us still so He could fix it. Nothing can happen that will surprise Jesus. It surprises us. It frazzles us, but it doesn't frazzle Jesus.

Is He trying to talk to you and you won't stay quiet long enough to hear what He is saying?

> Be still, and know that I am God; I will be exalted among the nations. I will be exalted in the earth! (Psalm 46:10 NKJV).

> Make it your ambition to lead a quiet life, to mind your own business and to work with your hands. So that your daily life may win the respect of outsiders... (1 Thessalonians 4:11-12 NIV)

> Instead, it should be that of your inner self, the unfading beauty of a gentle and quiet spirit, which is of great worth in God's sight. (1 Peter 3:4 NIV)

Chapter 11

One Step at a Time

YOU WOULD THINK that only one of my twins was hyperactive, but the fact is, they both could hold their own in any situation.

We were constantly in church, and getting the twins ready was a dual effort. We could only hope they wouldn't spill something on themselves or get too dirty by the time we got to church. I am sure that this situation is very familiar to all who have children.

At the time, we lived in a modular home with steep steps that led to the front door. My girls were approximately two-years-old by this time and knew the routine of going to church. I had the youngest and I was just a few steps in front of my husband who had the oldest as we went out the door. Suddenly, instead of walking down the steps, she decided it would be more fun if she flew.

My man, unknown to the thoughts in a two-year-old's mind, had her tightly by the arm so she would not fall down the stairs. She jumped, he jerked and she screamed.

A little back story is that my man played backyard football on Sunday afternoons with the other guys from the church, for as many years as his body could take it. He dislocated his shoulder and broke his collarbone during some of these "fun" afternoons. He was very aware of the sound a breaking bone makes as well as the look of one shoulder dropping below the other one.

He immediately scooped her up with the intent of going straight to the Emergency Room for the painful task of resetting her shoulder or collarbone. It was broken; no doubt about it.

However, since we only lived a few blocks from the church and believed in the healing power of Jesus; we drove to the church first with the intent of getting prayer and then going to the hospital. Can't say we had much faith, did we?

Is that an oxymoron or what? I have a little faith for prayer, but then we'll go on to the hospital.

Just a side note – I was playing with my older brother when we were children, and I fell off an inner tube that we were bouncing on and broke my arm just below the elbow. We were very poor and couldn't afford a doctor, so my parents prayed, and my broken arm was completely and miraculously healed. So I was very aware of what God can do.

Now back to my story. When we got to the church, the sweet early folks gathered around and began to pray for this screaming child. If you ever need prayer, call on the early folks. They have a good expectation of what God can do! Almost immediately, she stopped screaming and fell sound asleep, so we decided to skip the hospital and stay for the service.

Close to the end of the service, she woke up in pain, so we placed her in the car and began the trip to the Emergency Room. My dad drove, and I held her tight in my lap as to not move her shoulder/collar bone and cause her more pain.

The hospital was a good twenty-minute drive into the next town. As we drove, I was trying to explain to her just what would happen at the Emergency Room and to ease any fears she might have.

About ten minutes into the ride, she promptly told me, "Mommy, Jesus made me all better." I continued to explain how she didn't have to be afraid of the Emergency Room and the people there would make her all better. She repeated this statement numerous times, and I assumed she was just afraid. "But Mommy, Jesus made me all better!"

Little did I know that the faith of the child far surpassed my limited faith. I continued to hold her tightly as we entered the emergency room, and I signed her in and proceeded to take my seat in the triage area with all the other people.

After sitting tightly squeezed in my arms for about fifteen minutes, she began acting like a typical two-year-old who had sat still for as long as she could.

I gently lowered her to the ground so as to not jostle anything and expecting her to begin screaming at any moment. We noticed that both of her shoulders looked the same. She was not screaming and we began to notice that she was not only moving her arm but was moving that shoulder and not screaming.

From the time the twins were a few months old, if we wanted them to raise their hands, we would just say, "Praise the Lord," and they would raise their hands toward Heaven no matter where they were. As a Praise and Worship leader, what else would you expect from me except to teach them at a young age to Praise the Lord?

I said, "Praise the Lord," and up went both hands straight into the air as she continued to locate some toys to play with in the Emergency Room. As onlookers thought we were a few songs short of a hymnal, we scooped her up and walked out of the Emergency Room with the receptionist chasing us into the parking lot, trying to convince us that the wait would not be much longer.

We knew then that she had been completely healed in the car heading toward the hospital; we just refused to believe a two-year-old when she said she was "all better."

How many times is Jesus wanting to make us all better, but we discredit it because it doesn't happen the way we think it should?

Unbeknownst to us, the church had gathered one more time to pray for the little girl with the broken collarbone, and after praying, the evangelist made the statement, "Jesus just healed that child," and He did!

My daughter learned the hard way that despite what she saw on TV, she really couldn't fly, but she also learned that she serves a big God who is well able to heal her even when grownups just don't get it.

It wasn't my supernatural faith, I was not a super-Christian. It wasn't anything that I could do to make the miraculous happen. It was the mercy and grace of my Lord and Savior Jesus Christ and the faith of a child and a group of people who decided to pray just one more time.

As much as we as a family believe in divine healing, we also believe that we would not do anything to hinder the well-being of one of our children. Sometimes God miraculously heals, and sometimes He uses doctors to bring healing. Never jeopardize that.

However, never forget to pray just one more time. Is someone in the hospital? Is someone in the midst of a divorce? Has someone lost his or her home or job? Let's pray just one more time. While others are in their darkest hours, let us remember to pray for them just one more time.

Is anyone among you suffering? Let him pray. Is anyone cheerful? Let him sing psalms. Is anyone among you sick? Let him call for the elders of the church, and let them pray over him, anointing him with oil in the name of the Lord. And the prayer of faith will save the sick and the Lord will raise him up. And if he has committed sins, he will be forgiven. Confess your trespasses to one another, and pray for one another, that you may be healed. The effective, fervent prayer of a righteous man avails much. Elijah was a man with a nature like ours, and he prayed earnestly that it would not rain; and it did not rain on the land for three years and six months. And he prayed again, and the Heaven gave rain, and the earth produced its fruit. (James 5:13-18 NIV)

Chapter 12

Low-Maintenance Friends

I ONCE HEARD that a true friend is someone who knows you and still chooses to be your friend. It is a blessing to have such close friends. Although the miles separate us, I know that at any given time, I would drop everything to be by my friends' side, and they would do the same for me.

My close friends have been by my side through ups and downs. They have all had a profound influence on my life and my family, and I love them more than they will ever know. We rejoice together in triumph and cry together in trials. I rest in the knowledge that they are there for me at all times.

One such friend gave a name to our separated situation. She said we are low-maintenance friends. What a concept – friends who love you just to be your friend.

> A friend is not demanding and never self-centered
> A friend gives with no thought of getting in return
> A friend sticks closer than a brother (Proverbs 18:24).
> A friend will love you like no other
> Jesus is my best friend; everyone else is a benefit!

Are you the type person who can only be friends with one person? Do you not allow your friends to be friends with anyone but you? Are you a jealous friend? Do you get angry when your friend is a friend to others? Are you a friend only if everyone does what you want to do? Are you a friend only when the gifts are coming? I know people who are like this, and my heart breaks for them as they struggle for friendship.

We need to be true friends, not expect anything in return. I am blessed with dear friends who know my faults and still love me. My friends and I are happy to be low-maintenance friends. Are you?

> Greater love has no one than this, than to lay down one's life for his friends. (John 15:13 NKJV)

Chapter 13

Quick-Moving Fog

HAVE YOU EVER gotten yourself into a situation that wasn't bad when you went in, but somewhere along the way, something changed?

My husband and I have had the privilege of working with some great senior pastors; the greatest one being my dad. Although he did not have a college education, his wisdom was awe inspiring. He continuously studied and prayed and God blessed him with supernatural wisdom. He believed God's Word.

There is a saying that goes something like this. "God said it, I believe it, and that settles it." However, my dad would say, "God said it and that settles it – whether I believe it or not." Wow, what a faith.

On the flip side, we have worked with some men who allowed their own selfish desires or those of their family members to hinder the work of God in their lives.

There was a time when things got extremely difficult at one of the churches where we worked. We knew beyond a shadow of a doubt that God had placed us there. However, God knew that we would only grow closer to Him through the trying times. We were finally able to take a short vacation with our girls during one of these trying times.

We have always loved to ride horses and on rare occasions we would rent horses to ride. This was and is still one of our favorite things to do. The sad thing is, my body doesn't always feel like it was a good idea.

On one of these rare occasions when we got time off; we visited some friends in North Carolina. We found a stable. We went to check it out so we could ride the next day.

Riding horses is a beautiful way to enjoy the countryside and marvel at God's handiwork. The stable was located in what my husband called a "holler." A holler is a small valley located between two mountain ridges.

We went down the dirt road and walked around the lovely stable to make reservations to ride the next day. As we got ready to leave and made our way back to the car, fog had settled in on the mountain. We could not even see the road we had come in on. We had been there less than fifteen minutes when the fog rolled in.

I had never experienced fog moving in that quickly and that thickly. We were advised to leave before it got worse! As it was, it took us forever to inch our way back up to the main road and then inch our way off the mountain.

One minute it was clear, and the next, we couldn't see the road in front of us. Needless to say, we prayed and God guided us safely off the mountain.

Even though we had the honor of working with some mighty men of God, there were a couple of senior pastors who became jealous of our success with the youth. What an oxymoron. We are supposed to do a good job as youth pastors and then when the youth crowd outgrew the church crowd, we were treated poorly.

In each situation, God guided us out of the fog. One was actually fog and the other was spiritual fog. Although we loved all the pastors, there comes a time when we had to step away as to not be engulfed in situations that we felt were not ordained by God.

We pray that those who have lost their way will be led through the fog into His marvelous light; even if that sometimes is church leadership.

There is no place for unforgiveness and no place for bitterness in our lives; they only feed the fog. Unforgiveness and bitterness are like mixing smoke with fog. It's a deadly combination.

So many people have physically died thinking they were just driving into a little fog when in fact it was a deadly combination of fog and smoke.

Sadly, there have been church leaders whose ministries have crumbled because of the same mindset. They either didn't see or ignored the spiritual road signs that danger lie ahead. Because of this, their ministries were hurt. Maybe they thought that they had "driven" through spiritual fog before and this would be no different to only find out that it wasn't like anything they had traversed in the past.

The Lord brought the children of Israel out of captivity with fire by night and a cloud by day. What was light to the children of Israel was a wall of darkness to the enemy. I want to remain on the light side; don't you?

Whatever your fog or hindrance may be; slow down and inch your way through and always allow God to be your guide. He will see each of us through our times of fog.

Be still my soul and know that I Am God; I will be exalted among the nations, I will be exalted in the earth. (Psalm 46:10 NIV)

By day the Lord went ahead of them in a pillar of cloud to guide them on their way and by night in a pillar of fire to give them light, so that they could travel by day or night. (Exodus 13:21 NIV)

Then the angel of God, who had been traveling in front of Israel's army, withdrew and went behind them. The pillar of cloud also moved from in front and stood behind them, coming between the armies of Egypt and Israel. Throughout the night the cloud brought darkness to the one side and light to the other side; so neither side went near the other all night long. (Exodus 14:19-20 NIV)

Chapter 14

Hidden Worms

I HAD ONLY been married for a few years when we bought a small modular home. We purchased the lot and had the home placed on it. The lot needed a lot of work. Weeds were flourishing and no grass would grow.

We saved and saved and finally had enough money to purchase and sod the front yard with St. Augustine grass. We didn't want just any grass; it had to be good grass. All the preparations were made. We tilled up the soil, smoothed it out, and placed the large sod squares to fill the front yard with beautiful grass. Then we watered and watered and watered the grass.

For about a month, we watered and watered and then brown spots began to appear. We thought we hadn't watered it enough and we watered it even more. A few weeks later and our yard was totally brown and dead. Come to find out, gluttonous bugs had thoroughly enjoyed our yard and all the water.

I could just picture those bugs gorging themselves on our lawn, thanking us for all the water, which only made the grass easier for them to eat.

It was hundreds of dollars down the drain and a lesson well learned that we will never forget. Kill the bugs first, treat the ground, and then plant/lay the grass. Seems so simple now, but it wasn't back then.

How many of us feel like we have been planted into the area God has for us? We are growing and looking good on the outside. Then we discover in a short while that the bugs we forgot to treat are eating us up from the inside out.

The Lord wants us to kill the bugs in our lives before they devour everything He has planted within us.

Some marriages, friendships, and finances have taken a bite from a life worm that wasn't dealt with until it was too late. The only way to deal with a life worm is through much prayer and fasting and reading God's Word. In addition, there is nothing wrong with getting counseling.

Don't think that just because you don't see the worm that it has stopped chewing. The ones we don't see can cause the most harm, especially if they are not dealt with. I know what the worms are in my life, and I know it is only by the grace of God that He has helped me get rid of them.

What does your worm look like? Is it anger, depression, sickness, poverty, unforgiveness, selfishness, pride, self-righteousness, etc.? The worm needs to die. Kill the worm that is robbing you of what God has in store for you. You will not only grow spiritually, but your marriage, friendships, and finances also will grow and be healthy.

Oh yeah, and don't forget to water!

> "Listen! Behold, a sower went out to sow, and it happened, as he sowed, that some seed fell by the wayside; and the birds of the air came

and devoured it. Some fell on stony ground, where it did not have much earth; and immediately it sprang up because it had depth of earth. But when the sun was up, it was scorched, and because it had no root, it withered away. And some seed fell among thorns; and the thorns grew up and choked it, and it yielded no crop. But other seed fell on good ground and yielded a crop that sprang up, increased and produced some thirtyfold, some sixty, and some a hundred." (Mark 4:3-8)

Chapter 15

Coloring

Wouldn't it be a dull world if all the colors in the crayon box were the same color? Can you imagine all the beauty that comes with the season of fall if all the trees were the same color? What if every color was green?

The sky was green, the trees were green, all the houses were painted green, all cars were green and the ocean and all the rivers were green. It is almost too much to comprehend, no variance of color.

I have watched time and again, the gift of glasses for those who are color blind, and the reaction is heart wrenching. Watching them as they are seeing a world of color for the first time and the tears that begin to flow is an awesome experience.

While pondering this thought – you might think this chapter of my devotional is about racism. But this goes so much deeper.

I am thankful for all the wonderful colorful people that Jesus has placed on this planet.

I also have discovered that inside of all those colors there is a heart, lungs, kidneys, and several vital organs. In addition, we each have the same number of bones.

And to top it off – when we bleed – we all bleed red.

So as thankful as I am about this vast colorful world – I am just as excited about the sameness in each of us.

So many people describe themselves as non-racists and yet they have no tolerance for people with various challenging personalities. That one is too loud, that one is too shy, that one is too fat and that one is too skinny. I have discovered that people are a reflection of their environment.

I was married to the greatest man on earth before the Lord moved him to Heaven. He was an example of how you can overcome your environment. Although your environment may influence your life; it can make you better or bitter. He chose to learn from the good, the bad and the ugly of his childhood and through it all he chose to be like Jesus.

The bad and the ugly taught him how he did not want to live and the good, he chose to make himself even better.

If everyone would strive to be a reflection of the SON, this world would be a better place to live. Enjoy and embrace all the colors of skin, personalities, and uniqueness that God has placed in each one of us. Truly know that you are fearfully and wonderfully made.

> I praise You because I am fearfully and wonderfully made. (Psalm 139:14 NIV)

> So God created man in His own image, in the image of God He created Him; male and female He created them. (Genesis 1:27 NIV)

Chapter 16

You Can't Wipe Off Love

I COME FROM a strong southern family. The best way to describe us would be to compare us to a strong Italian family. There must be Italian in our heritage somewhere.

While growing up we were not always able to attend every family reunion; however, the ones we attended were filled with love and now I have precious and treasured memories of those times.

Our extended family was always full of kisses and hugs. I had a cousin that was just full of personality. She just lit up every room she entered. Every time she saw us, she would give us a big hug and a big kiss on the cheek. She also was known for her bright red lipstick which would remain on our cheek after the kiss. She was always gracious and would wipe the lipstick off after the kiss. I am truly blessed with a family who loved each other.

As my children were growing up, I would always give them a big hug and a kiss on the cheek (minus the bright red lipstick). Bright red just isn't my color.

Now that I have grandchildren, I do the same thing to them. My youngest grandson thinks it is cute to wipe off all my kisses. He has done this to everyone ever since he was very small (not just my kisses).

The last time he did this, I got a revelation that I knew was from God. I told him that he could try to wipe off my kisses. He could even get a shower and try to wash them off. However, he could never wipe off my kisses because they were filled with love and you can't wipe off love.

No matter how many times Jesus kisses us on the head and we try everything within our power to wipe off His kisses – they can never be wiped away. There is nothing we can do to stop His love for us.

I am reminded of the below scripture:

> And I am convinced that nothing can ever separate us from God's love. Neither death, nor life, neither angels, nor demons, neither our fears for today nor our worries about tomorrow – not even the power of hell can separate us from God's love. No power in the sky above or in the earth below – indeed, nothing in all creation will ever be able to separate us from the love of God that is revealed in Christ Jesus our Lord. (Romans 8:38 & 39 ESV)

Chapter 17

True Love

NOT ONLY DO I come from a loving family – I also come from a long line of very strong women. I am so blessed to have had the influence of my grandmothers and my mother and women who were like a mother to me.

Through the lives they lived and not just the words they said; I am who I am today. I pray I can leave that kind of legacy for my children and grandchildren as well as others I meet.

My aunt who is now in her 90s recently told me a story that I remember my mother telling me years ago and I am so glad she reminded me of it.

My grandmother was a tiny little strong precious woman. She practically raised eight children by herself as my grandfather died when she was in her early 40s and she still had children in her home.

She, along with others in her neighborhood would have to take the bus to town to buy groceries, etc. Some of her neighbors were very poor and worked very hard at picking oranges in Florida. Thy also had to take the bus to town to get what they needed for the week.

It was not unusual, in those days, for the mother to leave the smaller children with the older children to watch while they made their short bus trip to town to get groceries and return quickly.

There was a family of color that lived near my grandmother. The mother had taken what should have been a short trip to town; but the bus broke down while they were in town and left her stranded for hours. The sad part is, she had a nursing baby at home and she could not return to feed her baby.

The older siblings did what they could to pacify the baby in hopes that their mother would return soon. After many hours – the baby was getting extremely hungry, and the children were unable to console this precious crying baby. In addition, they had nothing in the house to feed the baby.

In desperation, they took the baby to my grandmother's house in hopes that she may have had something there to feed the baby until their mother was able to return home.

My grandmother who is of Scottish, English decent, took this baby of color and began breastfeeding him. No thought of color, no thought of any other way to handle the situation. This precious child needed to be fed and my grandmother had the means to feed him.

I was raised to love everybody, and skin color is just skin deep. What makes a person good or bad comes from the heart, not the skin. Jesus died for all. I'm so glad that He made us all beautiful in His sight. Skin color is like flowers – they are each beautiful and unique and God's perfect creation.

I spoke with someone recently in my office as they were discussing racial issues. My statement was "sugar is sweet no matter what color it is." If you hand me a baby, I'm gonna love on him/her and get lots of sugar and precious giggles. This is what I believe with all my heart and that will never change. There is nothing sweeter than baby sugar.

Oh if we could just love as Jesus loved.

> Then the King will say to those on his right, 'Come, you who are blessed by My Father; take your inheritance, the kingdom prepared for you since the creation of the world. For I was hungry and you gave me something to eat. I was thirsty and you gave me something to drink. I was a stranger and you invited me in. I needed clothes and you clothed me. I was sick and you looked after me, I was in prison and you came to visit me.' Then the righteous will answer Him, 'Lord, when did we see you hungry and feed you, or thirsty and give you something to drink? When did we see you a stranger and invite you in, or needing clothes and clothed you? When did we see you sick or in prison and go to visit you?' The King will reply, 'I tell you the truth, whatever you did for one of the least of these brothers of mine, you did for me.' (Matthew 25:34-40)

Chapter 18

It's A Matter of Choice

I HAVE LEARNED that laughter and learning to laugh at yourself and yes even laughing at others is truly healing. I have enjoyed and cherished every youth trip we have taken with our students. We have not always enjoyed the chaperones, but we have no problem, dealing with the students. However, we have had problems with the adults who act like babies.

Because of grown-up complainers, we developed a rule that on youth trips, we do not allow any negative talk – no complaining and no fusing. It teaches people that they can watch what they say, and we can teach ourselves, with help from God, to talk nice and to have a good attitude.

Even with this rule, there are adults who still complain and speak negatively, because that's what is in their hearts and they seem to like it that way. That may seem harsh, but the truth will set them free.

Attitudes are developed. You choose whether to have a good attitude or a bad one. Before we developed that rule, we were on a youth trip where a couple of adults had bad attitudes. Please remember, the bad attitudes came from chaperones, and not from youth.

On one such trip, we took youth to North Carolina to go snow skiing. We were blessed to have a young man who is now a pastor at a very large church in California with several sister churches. May God continue to bless him.

This young gentleman had such a contagious great attitude. I will always be grateful for his attitude that shone far above all the complaining chaperones. He left such a lasting impression on all the students, and they still speak of his influence today.

However, with all of his enthusiasm, he didn't know how to snow ski. Believe me; he didn't let that slow him down. After this young gentleman showed his ability to not know how to ski, we developed a new rule; everyone who goes skiing with us is required to attend ski school until they get it, no matter how long that takes.

He would go up the hill, and the first few times we saw him come tumbling down, we were terrified. However, he was an adult, over eighteen, and made his own decisions. In hindsight, God had to have had His hand on him for what was awaiting him in the future as a pastor. The Lord knew he had many more souls to touch and lead to Jesus.

We knew, by his lack of skiing style, who it was coming down the mountain. Sometimes his skis would arrive first and then he would come sliding after them. Other times he would arrive first and his skis would be chasing him. No matter what – he had the greatest attitude and was just so much fun to be around.

There were youth with us who were beginners and youth who were advanced skiers. We watched them throughout the day as they came down the slopes.

We noticed that there was a large mesh "slow" sign on the slope where two slopes joined (the beginner slope and the advanced slope.)

Then here came this awesome young man of God who was slalom skiing, because his other ski had beat him to the bottom. Did I mention that he was wearing the "slow" sign that he had taken out on his way down? It's a picture I will never forget as he came down the hill with that slow sign draped around him, flapping in the wind.

Youth, who are now grown, still talk about him and the lasting impact he had on their lives. What kind of impression are you leaving on others? Good attitude or bad attitude – it's a matter of choice.

> Do everything without complaining or arguing, so that you may become blameless and pure, children of God without fault in a crooked and depraved generation, in which you shine like stars in the universe. (Philippians 2:14-15 NIV)

> Finally, brothers, whatever is true, whatever is noble, whatever is right, whatever is pure, whatever is lovely, whatever is admirable – think about such things. (Philippians 4:8 NIV)

Chapter 19

Life According to Matthew

THIS BOOK WOULD not be complete without adding "Life According to Matthew." As I write this, I understand that most people will believe I am speaking of one of the apostles. Although I find the books of Matthew, Mark, Luke and John some of the most riveting books in the Bible, I am speaking of Matthew from Alabama, not Matthew from the Bible.

As a preacher's kid or a PK, we moved more often than I would have liked and in one of those moves, we ended up in Alabama.

I was privileged to attend high school there. However, my dad transferred to another church in the middle of my senior year. Yes, there were loads of tears, and even some anger on my part that my parents wouldn't let me move in with some close friends until the end of my school year. They were and still remain like family to me.

We have shared some of our greatest triumphs and heartbreaks. Even though the miles keep us apart, we know that prayer has no boundaries. My best friend and I both married within months of each other, and soon after my wedding, my husband and I moved to Florida.

I write the following story with permission from my best friend and mostly in her own words. How could I pay such tribute without spoiling it by rewording what has truly come from her heart? It's a story of blessing, hurt and triumph, but most of all; it shows how much God loves each of us.

On December 4, 1979, a beautiful sandy blond-haired baby boy was born. His eyes were crystal blue. He was a little angel, a gift from God and they named him Matthew.

Matthew weighed eight pounds and seemed to be as healthy as any newborn. The delivery was somewhat stressful and there were times when Matthew did not receive oxygen. Little did they know this would cause Matthew to be slow and he would later be labeled. As months passed they thought they had themselves a quiet, well-behaved little baby boy.

On Matthew's first birthday, he did not walk or talk. However, since he was their first child, this did not seem to be a problem to them. Others around would say, "There is something wrong with Matthew," but my dear friend could not understand why anyone would even suggest such a foolish thought.

Their pediatrician made them an appointment with a bone specialist and advised them that sometimes these children never walk. However, they never gave up, and Matthew did walk by his second birthday. Matthew was nonverbal until he was about four years old, so speech therapy began. With lots of prayer and dedication, Matthew began to talk.

The pediatrician would always send them to specialists for testing. Each specialist would tell them what Matthew would never do. Doctors would tell them they needed to get used to the idea that he was not "normal." They said that my dear friend and her husband needed to realize he would never be able to live a "normal" life. One specialist told them he would never ride a bicycle, never read, and never be able to bathe himself, nor would he ever be able to get a job and function in this world.

When they would return home from those office visits, his mom and dad would never cry or talk about what was said about Matthew. Instead, they went out and bought him a tricycle. One day Matthew went outside to play and they noticed that he was pedaling his tricycle by himself. They were ecstatic.

One summer the church they were attending at the time, held a six-week revival. Matthew was about eight years old at the time. The evangelist preached on "How Big is Your God?" Matthew went down to the altar to be prayed for. He told the evangelist that he needed a new brain and they prayed for him. When school started back that next fall, his teacher could not believe how much Matthew had learned over the summer. Matthew's reply was, "Well, I got a new brain this summer."

Matthew can read and held down a job for many, many years. Matthew received a miracle from the Lord and we have been learning from him ever since that time. His wit and wisdom is truly enlightening and we give God all the glory.

God can give us a new brain too, if we ask Him.

> Do not conform to the pattern of this world, but be transformed by the renewing of your mind. (Romans 12:2 NIV)

> I can do all things through Christ who gives me strength (Philippians 4:13 KJV)

Chapter 20

Tarry Until

HAS THE CHURCH of today lost the ability to tarry? Do we no longer know how to tarry? Or have we lost the desire to tarry until?

I've noticed, even in my own life, that when I am asked to pray for someone, I pray for them, right then. I call their name out to God to heal them and to give them strength for the battle.

However, when the sickness isn't immediately healed or when the battle seems to last a long time – my prayers seem to wane. I don't pray as earnestly as I did when the need was first brought to my attention.

Are we a generation who pray microwave prayers and then expect to receive microwave answers? Not all prayers are answered immediately. Jesus is not a genie in a bottle but our Lord and Savior.

You cannot stay on the frontlines and continuously battle – fatigue will set in. This should be the time when we as Christians, pick up the sword (Word of God) from our wounded fellow soldiers and fight for them, encourage them and love on them.

Oh, there have been so many times when I longed for someone to help me fight and no one showed up. Don't get me wrong – the Bible states that Jesus will fight our battles but there also are battles that we seemingly must face alone. God is always there, but sometimes friends are hard to find when you are in the heat of the battle. They mean well, they just have lives and battles of their own.

While my husband was alive, we went to dinner with close friends and family on a regular basis and even took mini vacations and trips together. Then when my man moved to Heaven and I began to be a full-time caregiver to my mother, the invitations stopped. It wasn't that they were being rude, things just changed. I had to learn to fight battles on my own. Although I depended heavily on my husband to help me fight or to fight with me; I had to learn to fight for myself and to depend totally on God.

In the heat of the battle can be a lonely place; but our Lord promised to never leave us nor forsake us.

> Be strong and courageous. Do not be afraid or terrified because of them, for the Lord your God goes with you; he will never leave you or forsake you. (Deuteronomy 31:6)

> So when the enemy comes in like a flood, the Lord will raise up a standard against him (Isaiah 59:19).

Jesus is always there beside us.

I am reminded of the old Andre Crouch song – Through It all, through it all, I've learned to trust in Jesus, I've learned to trust in God. Through it all, through it all, I've learned to depend upon His Word.

> ...in this world you will have trouble. But take heart! I have overcome the world. (John 16:33)

He is our strength, He is our comfort, and He hears our cries in the midnight hour when no one else is around. Loneliness can feel tangible, but during those times, I remind myself that Jesus stays closer than a brother.

> There is a friend who sticks closer than a brother. (Proverbs 18:24)

Be the friend who sticks closer than a brother. Be the friend who will tarry until the answer comes. When Jesus answers quickly or when it takes a while for us to see His hand in the situation; don't ever lose the ability to "Tarry Until."

The old timers used to call it "praying until you have prayed through." Be prepared to pray through – however long that takes! I encourage you to not give up but Tarry Until!

Chapter 21

What is that Wonderful Fragrance?

My daughter was working at our church's learning center and returned to tell us about one of the most beautiful students she had the privilege to meet. She said the child was a typical four-year-old; however, the student was legally blind. When my daughter would enter the Learning Center to perform her duties as an administrator, this child would come close and smell her, and then say "Hi, Ms. Valerie, where's your baby?" The child recognized people by their smell.

As my daughter shared this touching story with me, I was taken back in time to another story that was all about a fragrance.

I was a daddy's girl from as far back as I can remember. We did everything together. I went fishing with him and played ball with him and he taught me how to swim. I was his caddy on the golf course and traveled with him to his preaching engagements. I'm not sure if he ever tired of his shadow, but I was always there by his side. I was even privileged to watch as a host of angels carried him home on the day he moved to Heaven and took his last earthly breath.

I was grown and had grown children of my own when he moved to Heaven. I thought my world had crashed in around me when he died. Seven years after his death, as we were moving, we came across some of his old cologne.

As we opened the bottle of cologne, I was instantly taken back to the rear of the church where, as a minister, he would stand, following every service, and shake hands with all who had come. I would shake hands with him just so I could smell his fragrance on my hands.

I also was reminded of the smell of his cologne that would fill the house early on Sunday mornings as he got all dressed up for church.

It's amazing that just opening that old bottle of cologne brought back such joyous memories. It still smelled just like him even after all those years.

Later that week as I prepared a blueberry cake to take to a work luncheon, I was told that if I brought it, it must be "very sweet" not because I am a good cook, but because of my attitude at work.

It made me ponder; what kind of fragrance or taste do people associate with us? Do we have a bad attitude that brings a sour smell when we enter or leave a room? Does what we bring to the table taste bitter, rotten and spoiled, or is it sweet and refreshing?

Our attitudes should be such that we leave a pleasant fragrance so that years from now, long after we've moved away, people will remember the pleasant fragrance of our lives.

Do you have a rose-like attitude that when the pressure of life seems to crush us, the more we are crushed, the more beautiful we smell, just like a rose? Are you the rose with one of the most beautiful fragrances on the planet, or are you more like the stem? Do you leave a sweet spiritual fragrance, or do you just stick everyone who gets too close?

It's all about our spiritual smell. It's not so much the one we spray on the outside of our bodies, but the one that fills our spirits. It's all about the smell that remains long after we are gone. It's all about attitude. I choose to have a sweet one.

> For we are to God the aroma of Christ among those who are being saved, and those who are perishing. (2 Corinthians 2:15 NIV)

> To be made new in the attitude of your mind (Ephesians 4:23 NIV)

> And live a life of love, just as Christ loved us and gave himself up for us, as a fragrant offering and sacrifice to God. (Ephesians 5:2 NIV)

> If you have any encouragement from being united with Christ, if any comfort from His love, if any fellowship with the Spirit, if any tenderness and compassion, then make my joy complete by being like-minded, having the same love, being one, in spirit and purpose. Do nothing out of selfish ambition or vain conceit, but in humility consider others better than yourself. Each of you should look not only to your own interests, but also to the interest of others. Your attitude should be the same as that of Christ Jesus. (Philippians 2:1-5 NIV)

Acknowledgements

FIRST AND FOREMOST, I want to thank my Lord and Savior Jesus Christ, for without Him I would not be alive. He is the very air I breathe.

I want to extend a special thank you to my husband who is now in Heaven, but encouraged me to write this book and take this journey. He was my strength, my stability, my rock and my best friend. He preferred to stay behind the scenes; however, I admired His God-given gift of knowing just the right thing to say. His advice and wisdom were truly gifts from God and are still ringing in my ears.

Thanks to my girls and their families who always seem to find humor at my expense. Thank you for your encouragement to me in completing this journey. You are my life! I am so proud of the mighty men and women of God you have become and the choices you have made. I thank God for placing you in my life.

Words cannot express the love and wisdom I have gained from my mom and dad. You are the greatest Godly examples of how to truly live Christ like. You have taught me that through giving, I am blessed. You are the most giving people I know. I pray that I can change lives the way you have.

Special thanks to my brother and his family who I love more than words. He has always encouraged me and always knows just the right thing to say to me to set me straight. And yes, he also finds humor at my expense. He has been my rock since my husband moved to Heaven and I could never thank him enough.

I also love all of my extended family and close friends. You have inspired me and allowed me to touch lives through my stories.

Special thanks to all the mighty men and women of God who have taught me all about the Lord and life! Thanks to all of my church family, here and scattered across the United States. I will forever remember the impact you have made on my life.

Last but not least, I want to thank all of the young people we have been honored to minister to throughout the years. Thanks for your youthful wisdom and for never allowing me to grow up. I am proud of all of you and the adults you have grown to be. Remember, you can do anything through Christ who gives you the strength.

Printed in the USA
CPSIA information can be obtained
at www.ICGtesting.com
CBHW071506200624
10388CB00006B/64